I

Your worst day

Imagine Listening

is our everyday...

RICARDO MARTINEZ II

TITLETOWN
PUBLISHING

TITLETOWN PUBLISHING, LLC

Imagine Listening
Your worst day is our everyday

TitleTown Publishing, LLC
P.O. Box 12093 Green Bay, WI 54307-12093
920.737.8051 | titletownpublishing.com
Publisher: Tracy C. Ertl
Editor: Lori A. Preuss

PUBLISHER'S CATALOGING-IN-PUBLICATION DATA:

Names: Martinez, Ricardo, II, author.

Title: Imagine listening : your worst day is our everyday / Ricardo Martinez II.

Description: Green Bay, WI : TitleTown Publishing, LLC, [2023] | Series: #IAM911.

Identifiers: ISBN: 978-1-955047-36-4

Subjects: LCSH: Police dispatchers--United States--Personal narratives. | Fire dispatchers--United States--Personal narratives. | Ambulance service—Dispatching--United States--Personal narratives. | Assistance in emergencies--United States--Personal narratives. | Telephone--Emergency reporting systems--United States--Personal narratives. | Emergency communication systems--United States--Personal narratives. | Public safety--United States--Personal narratives. | Crime--Sociological aspects--United States--Personal narratives. | Job stress--United States--Personal narratives. | LCGFT: Autobiographies. | BISAC: BIOGRAPHY & AUTOBIOGRAPHY / Fire & Emergency Services. | SOCIAL SCIENCE / Criminology. | BIOGRAPHY & AUTOBIOGRAPHY / Personal Memoirs.

Classification: LCC: HV7911.A1 M37 2023 | DDC: 363.2/4--dc23

Acknowledgments

9-1-1 professionals have historically been viewed as the most important person you will never see. They were on the back burner, the outcast of public safety. However, times have changed. At one time, it felt like they were not allowed to have feelings. They would answer a call, send help, and go right to the next one. No matter the situation, if there were no time to breathe, one would go to the next call. It can be a vicious cycle.

It is a new day for 9-1-1 professionals. They have gone from the most important person you will never see to the most vital piece of public safety. Truth be told, they always have been. The curtain has been pulled back, and they are sharing their stories. Every call starts and ends with these first responders. While most calls are horrifying, there are also good outcomes. For hours on end, they listen and send help. Some of those voices stay with them.

I want to thank the women and men of 9-1-1, the Thin Gold Line, for the job they do. Not many can do this job, and without them, help would not arrive in a timely manner. Their stories make up what is known as the #IAM911 movement. They have been shared all over the world and have opened the eyes of millions to what they do and deal with daily. Through the power of storytelling, they have helped many people heal and find some form of closure.

Warning: The stories you are about to read are all true and come from the 9-1-1 professionals who have lived them. If you have PTSD or suicidal tendencies, you are reading at your own risk.

I REMEMBER
THE SCREAMS

I REMEMBER
YOUR LAST
BREATHS

I THINK OF YOU
OFTEN, I
REMEMBER YOU

Welcome to *Imagine Listening –
Your worst day is our everyday.*
This is the beginning of a series
of books that will feature stories
from the #IAM911 Movement.

I *Your worst day*
Imagine Listening
is our everyday

IN THE MOMENT OF CRISIS I AM

THE VOICE WITHIN THE TRENCHES

I AM THE ONE
WHO KEEPS YOU CALM.
I AM THE ONE
WHO SENDS YOU HELP.
I AM THE NAMELESS,
THE FACELESS,
THE UNSUNG HERO
OF PUBLIC SAFETY.

foreword

At a pivotal time in my career, I learned about the #IAM911 movement and the Within the Trenches podcast. I was a 20-year dispatcher that had worked his way up to the administrative level of a countywide full discipline Emergency Communications Center. A dispatcher with 20-plus years of calls buried, buried pretty deep. Listening to others like me and reading their stories provided by the #IAM911 movement, I learned I was not alone. I quickly got hooked on the podcast, not just to hear the stories; it became a learning tool. I learned how other centers recruited and trained personnel and how they handled calls, but most importantly, we all learned it was okay not to be okay.

What is the worst call you have ever heard? A question we have all heard, and for some, our response is, "You don't really want to know." Your worst day is our everyday. Think about that for just a moment. It is no wonder we are in the highest understaffed public safety careers. It takes a very special breed to do what we do every day. Since the beginning, dispatchers have heard, "They don't get affected, they were not there, you were just on the phone, suck it up buttercup, or even, man up and just answer the phone."

So, we sit there wondering, did the boy survive? Did they make it out of the fire? Are my officers okay? We often go home never knowing those answers. All the while, we are just burying these calls deeper and deeper to make room for more. Well, even the strongest

dams fail eventually from pressure. Without the regular release of this pressure, something, more accurately – someone – is going to burst. I have firsthand experience with this need for release. Listening to the brave men and women of this Thin Gold Line family tell their stories, thousands of them, I learned I was no longer alone. But I was still reluctant to finally admit that I needed more than just a release.

As the #IAM911 movement grew, I couldn't help but think this is growing so fast, not just because we finally had a way to vent, but the way we were able to vent. The creator of the movement was one of us, a dispatcher like me that had listened to too many last breaths taken, too many screams for help, too many emotions, and no way to express our own emotions or perhaps even just cry. Those tears would say we wanted to do more but couldn't; the tears say I wish I could reach through the phone and just hug you or just say I'm sorry for what has happened.

As I continued to listen to the stories, I heard something else. Our host was relating to those stories. You could hear a sense of relief in his sometimes broken voice. That connection allowed us to open up even more and finally, for some, to get closure. I personally felt that connection. I learned how to release my calls finally and finally say I'm not okay. I learned how to release these calls to finally get them out of my head. The movement also taught me to search for closure in calls, not just for me but, more importantly, for my own Thin Gold Line family.

I know I speak for many when I say thank you, Ricardo, for giving us this opportunity to talk, to listen, and to learn – it's okay not to be okay.

Gary A. Hill
Warren County, NJ

We worked that day. A day that not many have experienced. We are members of an elite club...that no one wants to be in. We handled a school shooting. #IAM911 #ThisIsUs

same age as my sister. I'm glad I apologized for... I'm glad I didn't believe her, I'm glad she said all of that on a recorded line and I'm glad they were arrested for what they did to you. I am so thankful that you have family taking care of you. Your name is Superman, not for what they said you did but for what you overcame. Thrive on Superman, I'll never forget you.

OVER A NEARLY 13 YEAR CAREER, I'VE LITERALLY TAKEN THOUSANDS, UPON THOUSANDS OF CALLS FOR POLICE ASSISTANCE. SOME OF THOSE CALLS WERE EASY, SOME A LITTLE HUMOROUS, BUT MOST WERE SERIOUS IN NATURE. HOWEVER, A FEW VERY CRITICAL CALLS HAVE STUCK WITH ME. SO MUCH SO, THAT EVEN IN MY TIME OFF, THERE ARE TIMES THAT IT IS DIFFICULT TO TURN OFF THE MEMORIES. #IAM911 #THISISME

...ll hear quite a few of ...r voices in my head ...g after the call has ...ed, good and bad. I've ...n a lot of your stories ...me over the years. ...aybe I shouldn't have ...you've now become ...art of my life and I'll ...ver forget you. I just ...k of it as part of the job. ...AM911 #ThisIsMe

I trained her,
She has taught me,
Twenty-one years separate us,
The sounds of lives lost join us,
We have cried together,
Laughed together,
And celebrate the saves together.
We are co-workers,
We are friends,
We are in this together.
#weare911
#thisisus
#iam911

I've heard your first breath
I've heard your last breath
I've heard your cries
I've heard your silence
Your voices in my head are there forever.
#IAm911 #ThisIsMe #ThisIsUs

I answered when you took your last breath.
I answered when your baby wasn't breathing.
I answered when someone you trusted hurt you.
I've answered thousands of calls and they ALL have left their imprint.
#IAM9-1-1 #ThisIsMe

I still think about how I should have gotten units there faster. Maybe you'd still be alive. Instead, a man in white painters suit shot you as you were opening your store for the day, taking your cash bag. They still haven't caught him. I'm so sorry.
#IAM911 #ThisIsMe

I heard your last breath
the night you flipped your
four wheeler.

#IAM911

Introduction

Imagine watching your son take off on his four-wheeler. You have witnessed this many times. He rides, he has fun, and all is well. Now imagine you are 9-1-1, taking a call from frantic parents who have just found their son underneath his flipped four-wheeler. You listen to the parents scream while removing it off his body. You tell them that help is on the way, and you give them CPR instructions. An officer arrives, and you listen as he performs CPR.

"Come on, buddy. Come on," is what you hear over the phone.

This is what it is like within the trenches of 9-1-1, and this was a call I took. It is also the story to the left, the one that started the #IAM911 Movement on August 24, 2016.

When the movement launched, I was in Florida for the International Association of Public-Safety Communications Officials (APCO) conference and had heard about the reclassification issue that APCO originally started. They proposed that the Office of Management and Budget change 9-1-1 dispatchers from their current classification under "clerical" to the more appropriate "protective" class, the same as police, fire, and EMS.

The initial proposal was rejected, and APCO sent out a blast to its members, non-members, and the public to help push the issue. The National Emergency Number Association (NENA) joined the fight as well.

After looking at what both organizations were doing, I decided to insert myself into the

fight by focusing on one of the elements that both organizations were looking for — stories. They wanted stories from dispatch to show how they differed from commercial dispatchers and clerical workers.

Since I had been telling dispatch stories for a few years already, I felt it would be a perfect opportunity to assist. However, I wanted it to be an in-your-face look at what dispatch deals with. I wanted to be blunt, and I wanted to strike a chord.

The idea of this movement would be to take ownership of the story being told and, in conversation, reach out to the caller to say, "I am the one who was there with you." It would be a way to reach out and, hopefully, a way to gain some sort of closure by sharing the story.

It is a mere glimpse into the call I took when I heard this teenager's last breath. It's powerful. I will never meet the ones who called, but if they ever read this, they would know they were not alone. I am the one who answered their call. I am 911.

I asked others to do the same and share their stories anonymously to our inbox. I wanted to keep the authors anonymous because I wanted them to feel comfortable sharing their stories without feeling like they would get in trouble. Dispatchers don't always like to talk about their stories. Some of them hold it in for years. I know. I was one of them.

Overnight, stories poured in. I had four Facebook page admins, and I quickly added two more to keep up with the inbox. We were flooded with stories on Facebook, and I began to receive them on Twitter and see them tweeted and retweeted.

From what I was told, #IAM911 hit number three in the top trending topics on Twitter that weekend. It hit Canada and spread across the pond to the U.K. and even further to Australia, spawning #IAM999 and #IAM000.

The movement had busted at the seams, and the most important person you will never see was in the spotlight.

The stories were gut-wrenching, with some occasional happy moments. The majority are hard to read, but that's exactly what I wanted.

Stories also rolled in from the other side, too. These are stories from the callers giving their side of an #IAM911 story.

People were reaching out to the dispatchers who helped them. Even though they would never meet them, they wanted to thank them by sharing their story.

As the movement continued to explode, the news media took notice, and everywhere you looked, there was a news story on the movement and what it stood for.

For the first time in a very long time, they were reporting on dispatch from a different side.

They showed what dispatchers go through, the calls they take, and the stress of the job. This was needed.

Whether it was for the reclassification issue or not, it was needed.

I have read message after message from all public safety, not just dispatch, saying that they are so happy about the movement and what it stands for. Others have admitted that they have been holding in their stories for years and now have a way to get them out. The #IAM911 movement also shows how real PTSD in an Emergency Call Center is.

I have spoken to many dispatchers who have said that they suffer from PTSD. And even though reading the stories could be a trigger, it has also helped them heal and find closure by sharing their own stories.

What started as a way to raise awareness for the reclassification issue quickly turned into a

form of peer support. 9-1-1 dispatchers shared story after story and learned from each other. What did they learn? They learned that they were not alone. They learned that it was okay to feel instead of bury their feelings and stories, and by sharing their stories, the perception of what 9-1-1 dispatchers do and deal with was made clear to the public. This is important because people do not know or understand what it is like to answer a 9-1-1 call for help during a person's emergency, a literal nightmare. In the following pages, you will continue to learn from 9-1-1 professionals through the power of storytelling. While some stories have a good outcome, the majority are horrifying. This is their reality. Your worst day is their every day.

So, let's start with a bang. I want you to imagine each story. Become the dispatcher who has taken each call and imagine listening...

6 MINUTES WAS ALL IT TOOK FOR US TO BECOME FRIENDS
I TOLD YOU HELP WAS COMING.
I CARED ABOUT YOU.
MY OFFICERS HEARD THE SHOT.
YOU'RE GONE NOW.
I STILL CARRY YOUR DEMONS.

#IAM911

When you called me
all you told me was your address.
I called you back three times,
but you'd already shot yourself.
Mine was the last voice you ever heard.

#IAM911

You were with me from the beginning Grandma.
27 years later I took the 911 call... when you died.
How fitting to be there for me in the beginning
and I was there for you in the end.
I miss you Grandma.

#IAM911

I got a call from a man at the end of his rope. He was going to shoot himself because he felt like no one cared. I asked him what his interests were so we could become friends and I could help him get through his hard times. We talked for over an hour and had many things in common. Today, we've been married 23 years.

#IAM911

I HANDLED THE FIRE THAT TOOK YOUR LIFE, I WILL NEVER FORGET YOUR MAYDAY RADIO CALLS, NOT EVER.

#IAM911

I talked you through infant CPR,
including blowing rescue breaths
through the vomit that was still
in his mouth. He was blue when you
called, and we did everthing we could
but he was gone.

You were just the 15 year old babysitter.
Sometimes I wonder if you will ever
forgive yourself.

It wasn't your fault.

#IAM911

To a very patient & efficient dispatcher, I say....

You are the one person who has ever sent me a thank you. I've been doing this 9 years.
You reminded me of my own grandparents. I carry the card to work with me everyday. #IAM911

I listened to your broken
voice as you found your bride
of 50 years collapsed on the
bathroom floor... the same
month I lost my own grandma.
We got through 600
compressions together.
Your voice is still with me.

#IAM911

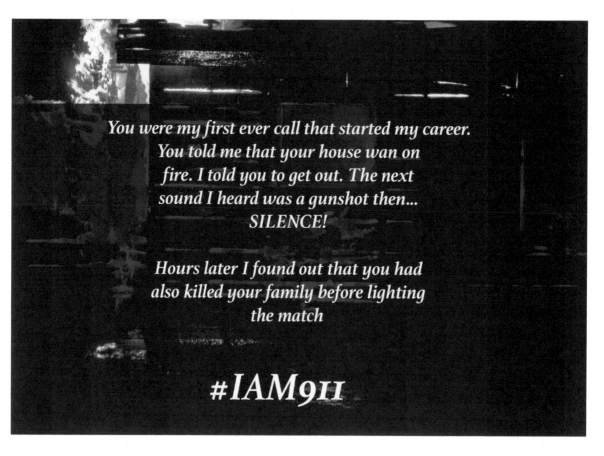

You were my first ever call that started my career. You told me that your house wan on fire. I told you to get out. The next sound I heard was a gunshot then... SILENCE!

Hours later I found out that you had also killed your family before lighting the match

#IAM911

I stayed with you on the phone, shaking, as you told me the details of your daughters rape. I went to the bathroom and cried for her. For you. I hugged my family extra tight that night.

#IAM911

I ANSWERED THE PHONE TO YOUR SCREAMS
BECAUSE YOUR HUSBAND HAD JUST SHOT
HIMSELF. YOU DIDN'T KNOW WHERE.
YOU DIDN'T KNOW IF HE WAS STILL BREATHING.
SILENCE CAME ABOUT, THEN I HEARD YOUR VOICE AGAIN.
I ASKED IF HE WAS BREATHING AND YOU SAID,
"NO, MA'AM. THERE'S NO WAY. HIS BRAINS
ARE SCATTERED ALL OVER THE YARD."
THAT WAS MY FIRST EVER SUICIDE CALL.
I'LL NEVER FORGET YOUR SCREAMS.

#IAM911

I ANSWERED 911 ONLY TO HEAR PRIMAL,
GUTTURAL SCREAMING... YOU CALMED
DOWN ENOUGH TO FINALLY TELL ME
THAT YOUR FIANCE HAD JUST SHOT
HIMSELF IN THE HEAD IN FRONT OF YOU
& YOUR CHILDREN. I'LL NEVER
FORGET THE SOUND OF ALL OF YOUR
CRIES AND I STILL THINK ABOUT YOU
AND YOUR KIDS. I'M STILL SO SORRY
FOR ALL OF YOU AND I STILL ACHE FOR
YOUR CHILDREN. IF I CAN'T GET IT OUT
OF MY HEAD - HOW CAN THEY?

#IAM911

I WAS ON THE PHONE WITH YOU WHEN YOU FOUND YOUR WIFE OF 10YRS HAD COMMITTED SUICIDE. I WENT TO HIGH SCHOOL WITH YOU BOTH.

#IAM911

#iam911

I listened as you made
excuses for why your husband
hit you, and heard your little
boy say he wanted to hit his
dad.

I was there when you found
your son had drowned in the water.
I have held you in my heart
since that day.

#IAM911

Your father found you in
the pond not breathing.
He sobbed as I talked him
through CPR that didn't work.
I can still hear him, I can still hear
your brothers screams.

#IAM911

I took your frantic
911 call and sent an
ambulance to help your
wife. She never met the
child I was carrying...
her granddaughter.

#IAM911

I stayed on the line listening to your
crying and timed 13 yr old voice
saying over and over
"It was an accident."
When you shot and killed your
11 yr old best friend

#IAM911

I hung up with you as you cried hysterically so you could call the right jurisdiction. It was a home invasion. You were 13 yrs old and home alone. You said you loved me and I you. I am a dispatcher. I am your Mother.

#IAM911

I sat on the phone with you for those last few seconds of your life, as you and your passengers screamed; they were the worst sounds I have ever heard. I could hear the flames roaring and then the line went dead. I hoped and prayed that you had made it out, but a short while later I learned that all 6 of you were killed when your suv overturned into that tree and engulfed. Still just a clerical position? #IAM911

I spoke to your quivering six year old voice, helping you hide your toddler brother and yourself while you listened and cried as your mothers boyfriend violently beat her. You were so strong, I told you what a strong girl you were, and how smart to call me, and to protect your tiny life and his. I pray you stayed a strong girl who will never allow yourself to be in a situation like that again.

#IAM911

I worked frantically for over
an hour to find you, even
though you made it clear you
only wanted someone to find
your life body.
#IAM911

I gave you instructions to control your unconsious mother's airway when her blood sugar dropped.
You were 7 years old.
You did a fantastic job.

#IAM911

I ANSWERED YOUR CALL ONE HOLIDAY SEASON. YOU WERE 17,
CRYING, STANDING IN YOUR BATHTUB FULL OF WATER, AND
HOLDING A HAIR DRYER. YOU SAID YOU DIDN'T KNOW WHAT TO DO.
BUT YOU LISTENED TO ME, LEFT THE BATHROOM, AND WAITED
BY THE FRONT DOOR.

I HOPE AFTER THAT NIGHT, YOUR LIFE BECAME EASIER
AND YOU FOUND PEACE.

#IAM911

I am the one that answered your call
when your 4yr old daughter was shot.
Your terrifying screams will forever be
with me.

#IAM911

I took your call when you were 10 years old and your 13 year old babysitter hung themselves in the kitchen while your parents were away. I told you how to cut them down and heard the thump as they hit the floor. After you said you couldn't do CPR I listened to your screams as help tried to find you. You didn't know the address but did an amazing job of attracting the police officer just like I told you.

I can still hear your voice and your screams. It's been 7 years and I still remember your name & pray you got through it and are coping...

#IAM911

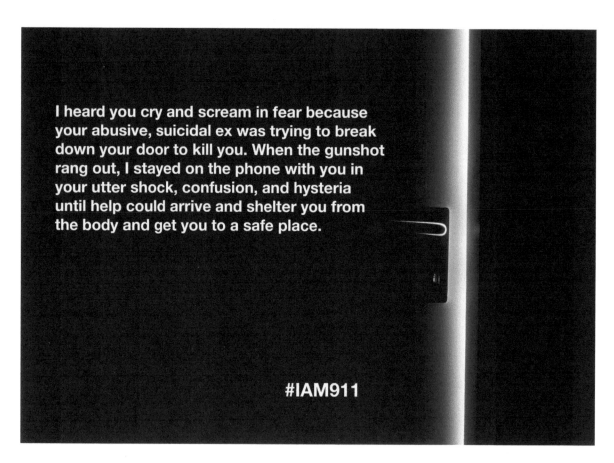

I heard you cry and scream in fear because your abusive, suicidal ex was trying to break down your door to kill you. When the gunshot rang out, I stayed on the phone with you in your utter shock, confusion, and hysteria until help could arrive and shelter you from the body and get you to a safe place.

#IAM911

I listened to you scream as your husband took his own life just down the hall from you. I stayed with you until an officer arrived to try to comfort you.

#IAM911

I SENT THE FULL ALARM AFTER THE FIRE ENGINE RESPONDING TO YOUR UNKNOWN MEDICAL ALERT GOT ON SCENE BEFORE EMS AND ADVISED IT WAS A WORKING FIRE. I LISTENED TO MY UNITS COMPLETE SEARCH AND RESCUE AND SAY THERE WERE 2 ELDERLY VICTIMS.

I WAS STILL IN TRAINING. AND I STILL BEAT MYSELF UP WONDERING IF THERE WAS SOMETHING I COULD HAVE DONE DIFFERENTLY SO YOU WOULD BOTH STILL BE HERE.

#IAM911

I STAYED WITH YOU ON THE PHONE FOR FIFTEEN MINUTES AFTER YOU FOUND YOUR SON HUNG HIMSELF.

#IAM911

To the dispatcher who answered my call when my one year old daughter went blue and lifeless and her eyes rolled back and she was gone for only seconds but what felt like forever... the person who calmed my screams and calmed my mother as she stood on the deck screaming for help, you put air back into my lungs and gave us infant CPR instructions and saved her. Thank you! My daughter laughs and loves and is so beautiful. She is here thanks to the dispatcher who took my call and helped us to help her.

#IAM911
from the other side

You were in your attic, and didn't have
a way out. You cried and begged me
to send someone. I told you I could just
get your address and send someone after
Katrina passed. The list was so long.
I still don't know if you made it out
with your newborn baby.

#IAM911

I walked into your room in the emergency department. You were disheveled, half drunk, and oh so angry. I asked if there was anyone that you wanted me to call. You snapped back, no, and told me to just fuck off and to leave you alone. I handed you a box of tissues and asked if you'd like something to eat. You threw the box across the room and demanded to go home. I asked you if you knew that you were crying. You looked at me and with a face of complete despair you said, "I can't stop."

I stayed in that room with you, talking about nothing, letting you vent, until they came to take you upstairs. You had dispatched emergency personnel to your own home two days earlier when your son called to say that your thirteen year old daughter had hung herself. I was the nurse that looked after her in the ER. Dispatchers are some of the toughest people I know.

#IAM911
from the other side

Reclassify PSTs
Within the Trenches Podcast
Join the movement

Blue face, cold to the touch.
I helped you with CPR after
you found your infant
face down, not breathing.
It messed me up...I did everything
I could but it wasn't enough.

#IAM911

I remember you... You were someone's grandmother and so we started calling you that when you called. I'm sorry you had dementia and had no idea you were calling us every night. I'm sorry your grandfather clock scared you every hour on the hour. I'm not sorry that I spent hours on the phone with you or that I asked you every time if you had eaten today. I know you are gone because the calls stopped coming, but I still think of you.

#IAM911

I kept you on the line as you whispered
"help me, I killed myself" over and over again.
When officers couldn't find you I used our
new map system to give them detailed
instructions until they found you hanging from
a tree. I wasn't leaving until they found you.

#iam911

I was on the phone with you while you drove home to check on your son. You were so calm telling me you received strange texts from him saying goodbye and he loved you. I listened when the shock hit as you found him bleeding from the head and the gun beside him.

You were still calm, describing to yourself more than me, what you were seeing. You thought he was still alive and breathing because his teeth clenched down on your hand while doing a mouth sweep and what would be his last breaths.

That hope in your voice crushed me because the moment you realized he was beyond help you cried to him, your baby you said. It took me long nights to get back to sleep right, although, nothing compared to your pain. I can hear everything today and hope you find strength to go on.

Just minutes before, my co-worker had been talking to your boy. She was desperately trying to find his location and get him back on the phone.

#IAM911

Before enhanced 911, when we only got phone numbers.
She called 911 and I spent 7 minutes listening to her be
sexually assaulted while I waited for the trace of
the phone to come back. I found out later that
the only reason the phone disconnected was because
he ripped the phone out of the wall to use the
cord to tie her up.

#IAM911

I was the one who talked to you when you were only 10. You were sitting by your mother's side, holding her hand after she shot herself in the head. You told me how much blood was there and how blue her lips were. You wanted me to make her wake up. I am so sorry I couldn't do that one request for you sweetheart. I wonder where you are today... 28 years later. I have retired my headset after 31 years but my memories never die. The hard ones are still with me still today.

#IAM911

I was once asked...

I was once asked...
 "Can you tell me what it is like to be on the receiving end of a 9-1-1 call?"

My response

Imagine your brother has been dealing with a bad breakup. You go to the bar, and after a few drinks, he tells you he wants to kill himself. You tell him to stop talking like that. It's not the end of the world. You head home, and when you arrive, your brother mentions suicide again. Fed up with what he is saying, you go inside, grab a gun and take it outside. You hand it to your brother and say, "If you really want to, then do it." You think that he will realize how stupid of an idea this is and will change his mind, but... he grabs the gun and shoots himself in the head, killing himself in front of you.

 Now imagine you're 9-1-1, receiving this call and only hearing screams. It sounds like two

females screaming over the phone. You ask, "What's your address? Ma'am? Can you hear me?" The screaming continues, and you type out, "Unknown situation." You remember a technique from your training and bring your voice to a whisper tricking the caller into thinking no one is there.

The screaming stops, "Hello? Hello?"

"This is 9-1-1; what's your address, and what is going on?"

While she tells you the address, you hear screaming in the background.

"I CAN'T BELIEVE HE DID IT! I CAN'T BELIEVE IT!"

"Who is there with you?"

"My boyfriend and his brother who shot himself outside."

"Who is the other female screaming?"

"That was my boyfriend..."

You realize the pain in the boyfriend, and although you are strong and calm on the phone, in the back of your head, all you can think about is your own brother.

"Ma'am, the police and ambulance are on the way."

"The ambulance is coming, okay?"

You hear your caller try to comfort her boyfriend, but you hear him yell something you will never forget.

"What the hell is an ambulance going to do? My brother's face is all over the snow!"

The screaming continues, and you hear your caller yell that her boyfriend now has the gun. He yells that he wants to kill himself. You tell her to get away from him, and he eventually drops the gun and runs back outside. The police arrive, and what felt like 15 minutes worth

of chaos was more like 3 minutes. Police secure the boyfriend outside and rush in to check out the caller. She continues to cry and says thank you. You hang up the phone and sit there in shock.

"Are you okay," your supervisor asks.

"Yeah, I'm good," you respond.

But you're not good. You're rocked, and the screams echo in your head. For the next 3 hours, they echo in your head, and all you want to do is call your own brother just to hear his voice.

When you finally get the chance, you tell him you love him. He asks what happened, and after you tell him about the call, he says, "I love you too."

This is what it is like to be on the receiving end of these calls. This was a call that I took, and this was years ago, but I can still hear those screams of heartache. It never goes away. It is always there, but you face it and manage it. I have said that taking a 9-1-1 call is like getting in a car, slamming the gas pedal, and letting go of the steering wheel. I used to bury these calls, and I caused more damage that way. Now I talk about them, and it's therapeutic for me. A big thing to understand is that 9-1-1 dispatchers are not drones. We don't JUST answer the phone. We are there with you throughout the entire call, and we may be calm and at the top of our game, but in the back of our minds, we are feeling your emotion. After the call, if there is time, we can reflect on it but the majority of the time? We pick up the next call and have no time to decompress.

I hope this answers your question...

Thanks, Ricardo

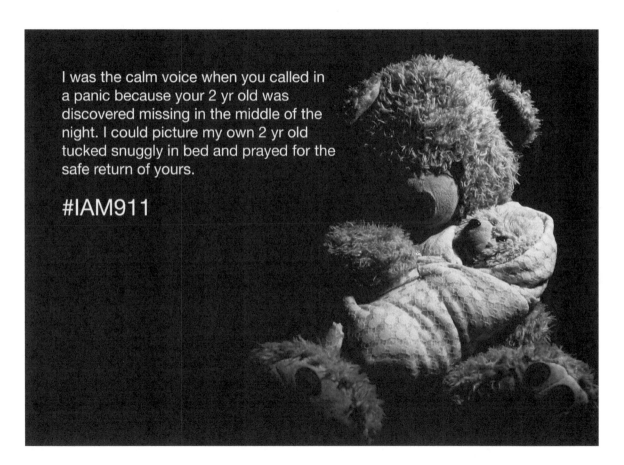

I was the calm voice when you called in a panic because your 2 yr old was discovered missing in the middle of the night. I could picture my own 2 yr old tucked snuggly in bed and prayed for the safe return of yours.

#IAM911

I was the last voice you ever heard
as your family's home went up in flames.
Your screams are forever in my memory.

#IAM911

I tried to decipher your emergency
through the screaming and crying.
Your neighbor was able to tell me
you found your husband hanging in
your garage. I'll never forget your cries
and despair.

#IAM911

I stayed on the phone with you after
you had found your father lying in the
hallway in his blood after you thought
he had hit his head.

When the paramedics arrived and rolled
him over they found the gun.
I heard your scream. You then asked me to
stay on the line with you until your
husband arrived.

#iam911

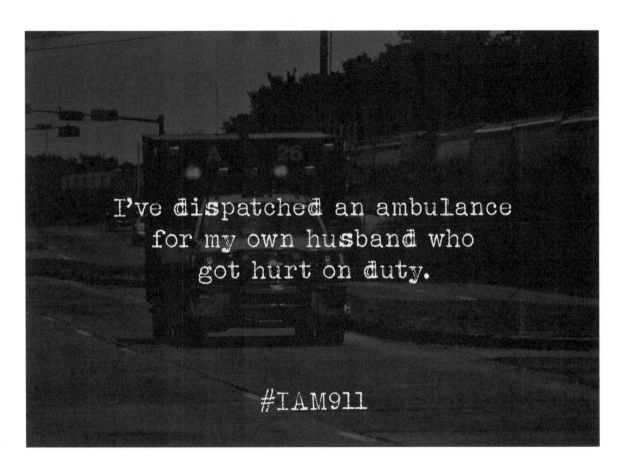

I've dispatched an ambulance
for my own husband who
got hurt on duty.

#IAM911

53

I kept calm and sent help while my officers listened to the shots whizzing past them and hitting things next to them. I kept calling your call sign waiting for you to answer, knowing in my heart you wouldn't ever answer my radio call again.

#IAM911

I remember your new wife's screams and frantic call on that September night. You had hung yourself in the barn after you and her had yet another one of your fights. I told her to cut you down with whatever she could find as I frantically typed directions to my old address. My world came crashing down. You were our daughter's father and I was your ex-wife.

#IAM911

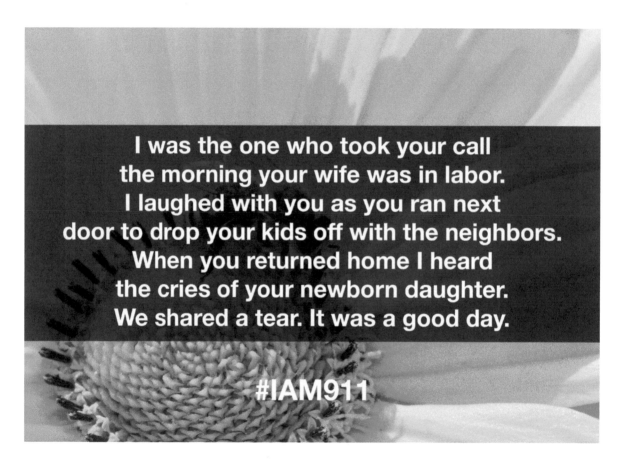

I was the one who took your call
the morning your wife was in labor.
I laughed with you as you ran next
door to drop your kids off with the neighbors.
When you returned home I heard
the cries of your newborn daughter.
We shared a tear. It was a good day.

#IAM911

You called and said you
wanted to kill yourself. I asked
if you had any weapons.
Then, I heard the gunshot.
That was 20 years go.
I still hear the shot.

#IAM911

I was the voice on the line when you called for help. You found your teenage daughter not breathing, and surrounded by unknown pills. You wanted to tell me all about her and I told you that her story wasn't over yet, and to help me help her. I told you how brave you were, as we counted through compressions together. I could hear my crew arrive and then the words I was waiting for, that she was breathing. I threw up thinking of the daughter I lost, and glad your story would end differently.

I went to our high school graduation 3 weeks later just to hear them say her name. I was just a face in the crowd, but I cheered for her. I heard the words "that's my girl" from the seats just 2 rows in front of me. I introduced myself after the ceremony and we just held one another and cried. I never told you about my little girl, but I was so glad you did not know that pain.

#IAM911

Your husband called for help at 2pm because he was worried that you may have bumped your head during a "fender bender" that you both were involved in. Together, after you both refused medical treatment, because everyone "felt fine," you went home. It was at 2am that you called for help because your husband woke you up by "making funny noises," and needed help. I talked you through CPR while thinking about how your daughter coached me for 7 years in several sports. I stifled my emotions when I remembered that my family was planning on attending your 50th wedding anniversary that weekend. I heard your husband's "death breath" escape as you became too exhausted to continue the CPR rhythm and then hit your fists on his chest before screaming and begging for him to wake up because you married him at 16 and you didn't know how to live without him.

Nearly 4 years later and I still randomly wake up in a panic because I dream about your screams as you bargain for the life of our loved one.

#IAM911

WHEN YOU DIDN'T ANSWER MY STATUS CHECKS ON THE RADIO I STAYED CALM. FOLLOWED PROTOCOL. DID MY JOB. WHILE YOUR BROTHERS IN BLUE RAN LIGHTS AND SIRENS TO YOU. I COULDN'T HELP BUT WONDER HOW I WOULD EXPLAIN TO OUR SON THAT YOU WERE NOT COME HOME.

#IAM911

Margaret, you couldn't breathe
and asked me to stay because you
were scared. I sat with you while
you took your last breathes. I cried.
You and many others live on in
my thoughts and will never leave.

#IAM000

I listened as you begged your daughter
not to die and to start breathing again.
She ate peanuts in a dessert and the epi couldn't
save her. I hear her sweet voice in my dreams.
We couldn't save her.

#IAM911

You were night fishing with your dad miles up a long, winding river. He fell out and never came back up. You called me for help, but I didn't know exactly where you were. I sent you a text from my cell phone so you could drop a pin using your maps app, screenshot it and text it back to me. I called you back and waited with you. I finally took a breath when I heard the boats. I still have the texts on my phone.

#IAM911

I am alive today because of a 911 dispatcher.
She spent a good amount of time talking to me about life
and after a while I put the gun down.
I would have comitted suicide if not for her.

#IAM911

I heard you trying to stay strong as you told me through tears how your drug addicted son just shot your husband in the head as he was driving down the highway...

You were taking him to rehab...

You did so well in staying calm so I could send help.
#iam911

You were lost, driving around an unfamiliar city,
with your boyfriend shot in the passenger seat,
frantically looking for a hospital.
I helped police and medics find you...too late.
I heard you become hysterical when
he died in your arms.
I've blamed myself for years.

#IAM911

I answered the call when a hysterical woman called
and said she found a teen in a vehicle
with a garden hose from the tail pipe going inside the car.
He wasn't breathing.
I walked you through CPR until help arrived 7 minutes later.
I left the office after that call was completed.
20 minutes later I held our mother while
she screamed and cried your name.
Your face and our moms screams still haunt me to this day.
RIP little brother

#IAM911

You watched your father shoot your mother and your 2 year old brother, then himself. You made your other siblings leave the house while you bravely tried to calm your brothers screams as you were instructed on how to control bleeding in between your own heartbreaking sobs. You were only 15.

#IAM911

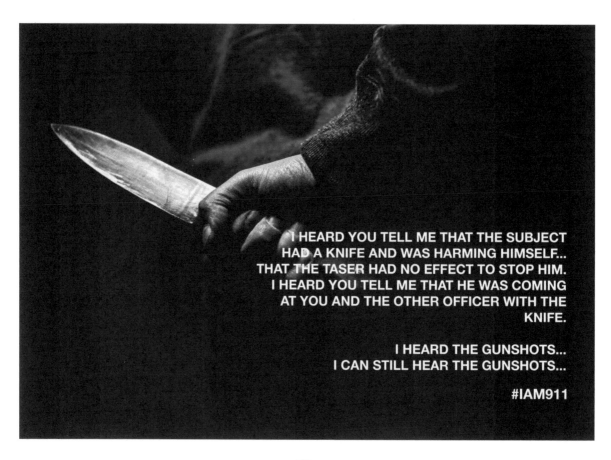

I HEARD YOU TELL ME THAT THE SUBJECT HAD A KNIFE AND WAS HARMING HIMSELF... THAT THE TASER HAD NO EFFECT TO STOP HIM. I HEARD YOU TELL ME THAT HE WAS COMING AT YOU AND THE OTHER OFFICER WITH THE KNIFE.

I HEARD THE GUNSHOTS... I CAN STILL HEAR THE GUNSHOTS...

#IAM911

I ASKED WHAT
YOU MEANT BY
"THERE WAS A SUDDEN
OUTBURST WITH KNIVES."
I FOUND OUT LATER
IT MEANT YOU
STABBED HER
ALMOST 30 TIMES.
#IAM911

I sent you help when you reported
your little boy missing...
Then stared into your eyes while
testifying during his murder trial after
you tortured and dumped him in
the canal before calling me...
#iam911

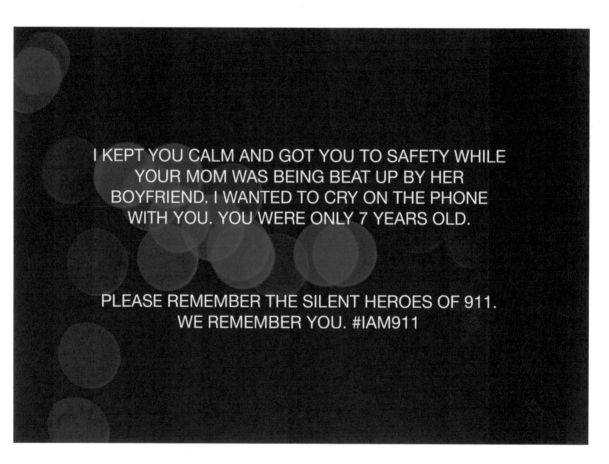

I KEPT YOU CALM AND GOT YOU TO SAFETY WHILE YOUR MOM WAS BEING BEAT UP BY HER BOYFRIEND. I WANTED TO CRY ON THE PHONE WITH YOU. YOU WERE ONLY 7 YEARS OLD.

PLEASE REMEMBER THE SILENT HEROES OF 911. WE REMEMBER YOU. #IAM911

I listened to a dad throwing up because he ran over his three year old daughter. I hear his wife in the background screaming, "You killed her." Yet I don't shed a tear. I'm numb to it all. Sometimes it's hard to turn the feeling back on when I walk out that door.

#IAM911

You were only 12 and the only other person home.
You woke up to find your dad bleeding from his head,
unsure of what was going on.
I helped you assess the scene, trying to protect you
as much as possible as from
what I thought the probability was,
but also trying to protect you from the possibility
of a danger of another suspect in the home.
I stayed on the line with you until officers arrived on scene.
Your dad had committed suicide for you to find him.
#yourvoiceshauntme

#IAM911

I took the call when your wife stopped breathing.
I'll never forget you pleading with her to not leave you.
I'll never forget dispatching EMS to our address
for your wife and my mother.

#IAM911

I listened to your last words, heard you yell at your dog to
get away from you, then listened to you shoot yourself.
You were only 17.
I later saw your suicide note on Instagram.
I still ache for your mom, who I understand
is also a single mom like me.

#IAM911

I told you everything was gonna be okay even though
I wasn't sure that was the case...
I told you how good of a job you were doing by talking
to me and staying calm as your body was stuck between a
truck and a tree. I begged you to talk to me again
when I heard you coughing and gasping for air.
You were 28 years old.
The medics pronounced you dead on arrival.
You will never know but I cried every night for a week
before bed because of you.

#IAM911

You were my last call of my shift. You called me screaming, hysterical.
You had just gotten home from taking your child to a friend's house.
You were looking for your dog's leash to take him outside.
You didn't expect to find your husband hanging from it.
I asked if you could safely remove it from his neck.
You couldn't.
It was New Year's Eve.
There's not a day that goes by that I don't think of you.

#IAM911

YOU CALLED 911 FROM YOUR CELL PHONE, GASPING
FOR AIR, TOO WEAK TO SPEAK. THE GPS PLOT
WASN'T ACCURATE. THE LAST THING YOU HEARD
WAS ME ASKING IF YOU WERE AT AN ADDRESS TWO
BLOCKS FROM WHERE THEY FOUND YOUR BODY TWENTY MINUTES LATER.
I STILL HEAR YOUR GASPS.
I AM SORRY.

#IAM911

I KNEW SOMETHING WASN'T RIGHT BY THE SOUND OF YOUR VOICE OVER THE RADIO. YOU DIDN'T HAVE TIME TO TELL ME THE PERSON HAD STARTED TO FIGHT YOU BEFORE I WAS ALREADY SENDING YOU BACK UP.

#IAM911

YOU WILL NEVER KNOW HOW MUCH
ALL FIVE OF YOUR LIVES MATTERED.
I SWEAR I DID EVERYTHING POSSIBLE TO
GET YOU ALL OUT OF THE BURNING HOUSE,
BUT IT WAS TOO LATE.

#IAM911

I am the one who heard your screams and last breath
as your 10 year old son called 911 as your husband
knifed you and clubbed you to death with a claw
hammer. It's been 15 years and I can still hear the
screams of your three small children
as I talked them into a safe area...

#IAM911

84

It was my first call after being cut loose, you told me that your son, who was a vet was walking around with a shotgun stating that it was a good day to die. You had barricaded yourself in the bedroom with your two grandkids and couldn't get out of the window.

I remember the fear in your voice and you begging him to get some help. I stayed on the phone with you for two+ hrs while passing info onto the TAC team. Everyone went home alive that night.

#IAM911

I am the first person you called when the neighbor boy came to your house because he accidentally shot his father on Christmas Eve. I was only on the job a month.

To this day, it is my saddest call.

#IAM911

I STAYED ON THE PHONE WITH YOU FOR 45 MINUTES WHILE YOU WERE TRAPPED IN THE WRECKAGE OF A 2 CAR CRASH UNTIL THE FIRST EMERGENCY UNITS ARRIVED ON SCENE. I HEARD YOU CRYING, I HEARD YOU SCREAM, "THE LADY IN THE OTHER CAR IS DEAD AND MY FRIEND WON'T WAKE UP!"

I FELT YOU DRIFTING IN AND OUT OF CONSCIOUSNESS, SO I ASKED YOU ABOUT YOUR FAMILY AND TOLD YOU THAT YOU WOULD MAKE IT HOME TO THEM, AND YOU DID.

#IAM911

You called 911 when you were feeling alone and suicidal.
We talked the whole time it took my officers to get to you.
By the time we hung up, you were telling me what you wanted to
study when you went to college. I think of you
every day and hope you're still alive.

#IAM911

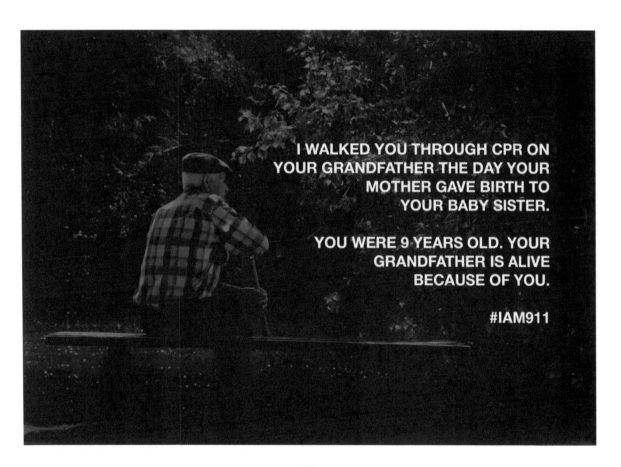

I WALKED YOU THROUGH CPR ON YOUR GRANDFATHER THE DAY YOUR MOTHER GAVE BIRTH TO YOUR BABY SISTER.

YOU WERE 9 YEARS OLD. YOUR GRANDFATHER IS ALIVE BECAUSE OF YOU.

#IAM911

#NeverForget911

24 hours later, calls were still coming in.
Many of you, I couldn't do anything to help but listen to you
until silence took over. 24 hours later, you were all still buried.
One call, 24 hours later, gave me the tiniest moment of happiness
I would feel for the next several days as more calls came in.
You were alive and miraculously, unharmed, just trapped.
For a moment, when you stopped speaking, I feared you had died.
I bawled like a baby when I heard the firefighters pulling you to safety.
You were the first call I took after the towers fell that didn't end with silence.
I never got your name, but I hope you are doing well.

#IAM911

It was a beautiful Sunday afternoon. Your husband and toddler were in the backyard "fishing" in the pool. Your husband saw the falling tree and rushed to your son. He was able to push him out of the way and the tree landed on your husband instead. He was bleeding from every oriface but he was still breathing. I gave you instructions to open and clear his airway. I sent you as much help as I could, including a helicopter. It wasn't enough. He died days later at the hospital. I think about you often and hope that you still find comfort in the fact that he saved your son. #IAM911

I WILL NEVER FORGET THE SOUND OF YOU TELLING YOUR 3 SMALL CHILDREN TO STAY INSIDE AFTER TELLING ME YOUR HUSBAND WALKED OUTSIDE AND KILLED HIMSELF.

I WILL NEVER FORGET THE MOMENT I REALIZED THAT HE WAS ONE OF OUR OFFICERS AND AN AMAZING FRIEND.

#IAM911

I answered the phone as your sister, just found out that you, her 15yo sister, had shot herself in the head. I assured her through her frantic and terrified sobs that help was already on the way to you. I did my best to try and calm her down because she was determined to get to you. She hung up on me to talk to your dad. I cried for you and her both on my 45 min ride home. I cried for your mom as I pulled my 18 yr old daughter into my arms and cried as I held her and told her I love her. I don't know your name, but I will never forget you or your sister.

#IAM911

I remember your screams
of agony when you
thought you were having
an asthma attack, you
were really having a heart
attack. I heard you take
your last breath on my
birthday.

#IAM911

You told me how scared you were that your mommy was getting hurt in the room next door. You did so good answering my questions and staying calm. You were 5 years old. We listened to the screams together. You were my hero that day.

#IAM911

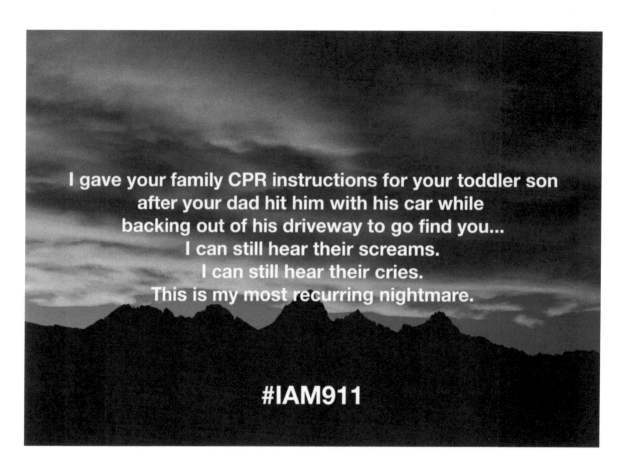

I gave your family CPR instructions for your toddler son
after your dad hit him with his car while
backing out of his driveway to go find you...
I can still hear their screams.
I can still hear their cries.
This is my most recurring nightmare.

#IAM911

Your usually very calm voice on the
radio was yelling in terror amongst the
splashing of water I listened...
HELPLESSLY at my desk as you
tried your best to save the
child from the pool.
Sadly, the child didn't make it...

#IAM911

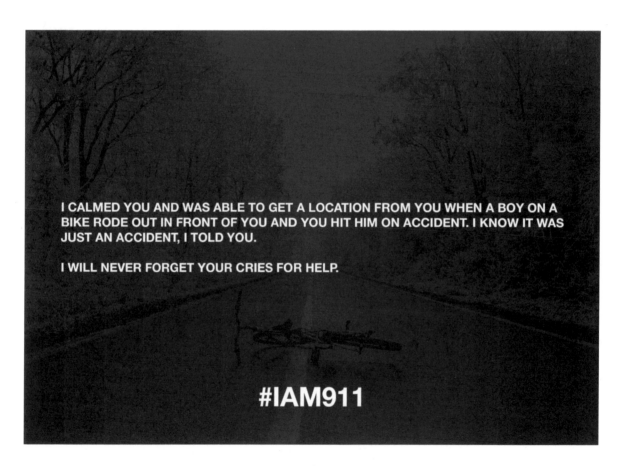

I CALMED YOU AND WAS ABLE TO GET A LOCATION FROM YOU WHEN A BOY ON A BIKE RODE OUT IN FRONT OF YOU AND YOU HIT HIM ON ACCIDENT. I KNOW IT WAS JUST AN ACCIDENT, I TOLD YOU.

I WILL NEVER FORGET YOUR CRIES FOR HELP.

#IAM911

I spoke to your son who had told me he murdered you. I sent responders and you survived 7 stab wounds.

#IAM911

Your wife went into labor and the baby was coming fast. You both did fantastic and I got to celebrate the healthy baby girl with you

#IAM911

I talked you through CPR on your
2 year old. You did everything right but
we couldn't get him back.

I share a bond with you not many
would understand.

#IAM911

Helping you cut down your 11 year old brother was the hardest thing I've ever done. I have an 11 year old son. My heart hurt while yours hurt.

#IAM911

YOUR AUTISTIC FRIEND CALLED YOU AND
SAID SOMETHING WAS WRONG WITH HIS
MOM. WHEN YOU GOT TO THEIR HOUSE, HIS
MOM WASN'T BREATHING. I STILL REMEMBER
HIS DESPERATE SCREAMS AND YOUR CALM
REASSURANCES TO HIM WHILE YOU DID CPR.
YOU DID EVERYTHING PERFECTLY, BUT SHE
DIDN'T SURVIVE, AND I'M SO SORRY.

#IAM911

The sound of your voice, asking for EMS to respond because your partner was just struck by a vehicle.What's worse was listening to the audio from the dash cams as you are asking calmly for EMS, and then screaming "NOOOO" as you run to his aid.
I will not forget.

#IAM911

You said you wouldn't make it to the hospital in time and you were right. Your wife was screaming in pain in the background. You not only followed my every instruction, but you also comforted her the best you could. Then I heard those sweet newborn cries... music to my ears! You did such a great job!

I hung up and announced to the room, "We have a girl!" This job is not all encompassing horror and pain. Although that is part of it, we experience victories too. Maybe it's the hardest calls that make those victories so much more beautiful and amazing. I'm blessed to work in this field with these great people.

#IAM911

You had been stung by a bee. You were alone, with no lifesaving medication. I comforted you, assured you help was on the way. I kept the responders updated. I heard your last words.
I heard your last breath.
I heard paramedics open your door.
I heard them call your name.
Moments too late.

When I wrote this, I was finally able to cry for you.

#IAM911

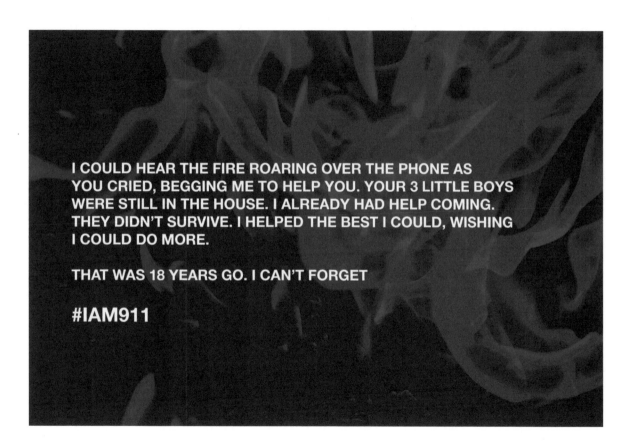

I COULD HEAR THE FIRE ROARING OVER THE PHONE AS
YOU CRIED, BEGGING ME TO HELP YOU. YOUR 3 LITTLE BOYS
WERE STILL IN THE HOUSE. I ALREADY HAD HELP COMING.
THEY DIDN'T SURVIVE. I HELPED THE BEST I COULD, WISHING
I COULD DO MORE.

THAT WAS 18 YEARS GO. I CAN'T FORGET

#IAM911

I'm severly depressed, utterly lonely and often feel suicidal. Knowing that I have helped people survive, comforted others in death and continue to help my fellow humans on the worst days of their lives is sometimes the only thing that keeps me going. Not many clerical workers can say the same.

#IAM911

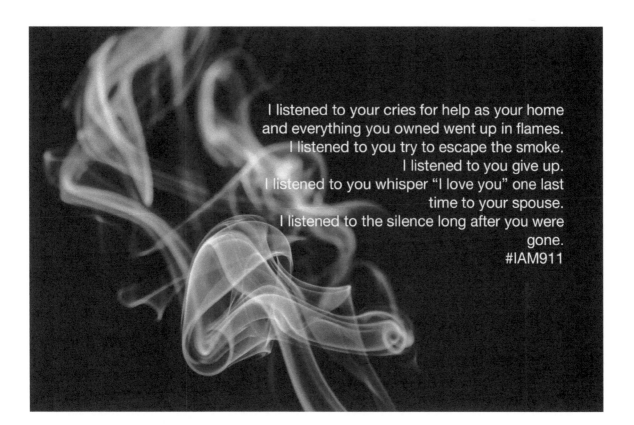

I listened to your cries for help as your home and everything you owned went up in flames.
I listened to you try to escape the smoke.
I listened to you give up.
I listened to you whisper "I love you" one last time to your spouse.
I listened to the silence long after you were gone.
#IAM911

You called to tell us you were speeding to the hospital
with your mother who was having chest pain.
I convinced you to pull over instead of driving recklessly.
Our responders got to you quicker than you expected.
You finally allowed yourself to relax. You didn't have to be strong anymore.
You thanked me for everything that we do. It was the first time
I had been thanked during a call.

You don't know I was silently crying with you.
Your words will stay with me forever.

#IAM911

You told me the CPR I was guiding
you through wasn't working and
it was my fault your brother was dead.

I BELIEVED YOU

You forgot to tell me you had beaten him
and shoved a tube sock down his throat.

#IAM911

Mine was the last voice you heard...
I can still hear you clicking.
I sent help to you.

I did the best that I could.
It still wasn't enough.
#IAM911

I answered the call from your sister who had found you after you hung yourself. She wanted to save you but you were gone. You weren't even 30 and you left behind two beautiful daughters. We played sports together and I was friends with your husband in school. Facebook blew up with news of your death. I wanted to cry every time your name showed up in my feed.

#IAM911

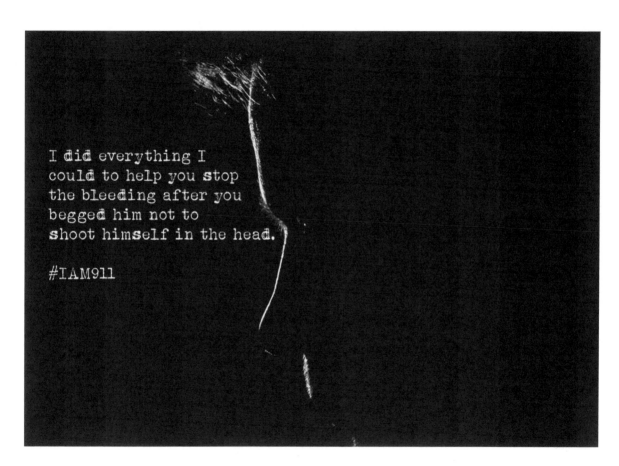

I did everything I
could to help you stop
the bleeding after you
begged him not to
shoot himself in the head.

#IAM911

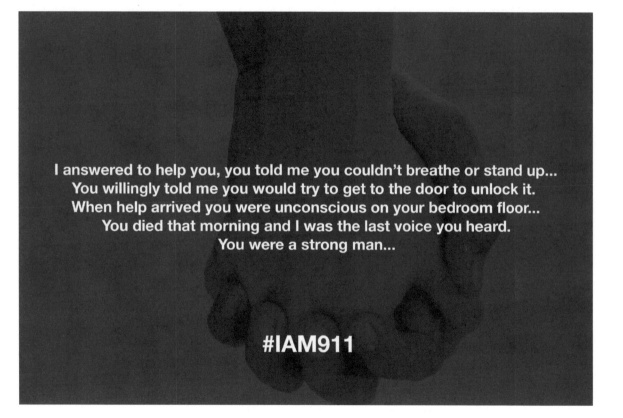

I answered to help you, you told me you couldn't breathe or stand up...
You willingly told me you would try to get to the door to unlock it.
When help arrived you were unconscious on your bedroom floor...
You died that morning and I was the last voice you heard.
You were a strong man...

#IAM911

YOUR SON HAD A TRAUMATIC BRAIN INJURY AND WAS COMBATIVE.
I STAYED ON THE PHONE WITH YOU AS HE RAN OUT INTO TRAFFIC.
I HEARD YOUR SCREAMS AND I WALKED YOU THROUGH CPR.
IT WAS MY FIRST NIGHT BACK FROM MATERNITY LEAVE. WHEN THE
PARAMEDICS ARRIVED WE CRIED TOGETHER AS THEY TOOK OVER.
I WILL NEVER FORGET YOUR VOICE.

#IAM911

I WILL NEVER FORGET THE EERILY CALMNESS OF YOUR VOICE THE NIGHT YOU KEYED UP ON THE RADIO TO ADVISE YOU HAD WALKED IN ON A ROBBERY IN PROGRESS AND WERE SHOT IN THE FACE.

EVEN THOUGH RESCUE WAS ABLE TO GET THERE IN TIME, AND YOU ARE BACK ON THE STREETS, EVERY TIME YOU KEY UP MY HEART SKIPS A BEAT.

#IAM911

IT WAS ME THAT HEARD YOU DROP THE PHONE AND SCREAM WHEN YOU FOUND YOUR TWO GRANDCHILDREN HAD BEEN SHOT TO DEATH BY THEIR OWN FATHER WHILE THEIR MOTHER WAS AT WORK.

BECAUSE OF THIS I WILL NEVER BE ABLE TO COMFORTABLY LEAVE MY SON WITH HIS FATHER, MY HUSBAND, WHILE I GO TO WORK. IT'S NOT THAT I DON'T TRUST MY HUSBAND WITH OUR SON, BUT THEIR MOTHER TRUSTED HER HUSBAND AND HE STILL DID THE UNTHINKABLE.

#IAM911

You had just delivered your baby. When you called 911 he was in the toilet and not breathing. You didn't think you could do it, but you did. We did. I can still hear his very first cry.

#IAM911

I talked to your wife as she tried desperately to keep
you alive after you shot yourself. I walked her through
the steps to try and control the bleeding. It broke my heart
to hear her telling you to pray. After it was over
I had to go to the bathroom and pull myself together
to be able to finish the shift. It was one of the first calls
my trainee tried to take.

#IAM911

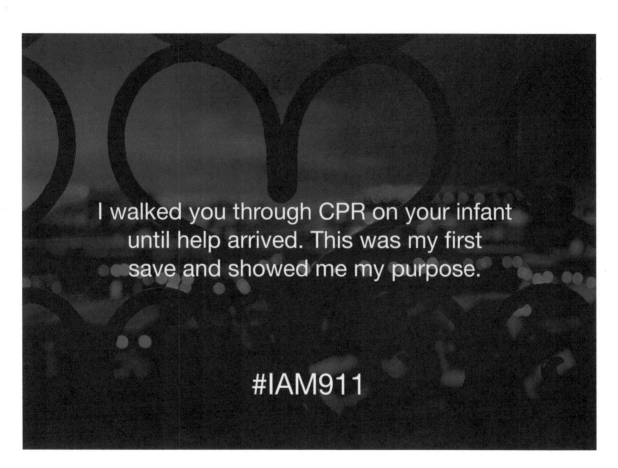

I walked you through CPR on your infant until help arrived. This was my first save and showed me my purpose.

#IAM911

I remember the tone of your voice sounded panicked, but almost inconvenienced. I remember you telling me she wasn't breathing. You said you didn't know what was wrong, but she just stopped breathing. I gave you CPR instructions, encouraged you, and did my best to keep you going, to keep her going. As soon as officers and EMS got there, I found out you were lying the whole time. You never even started CPR. You killed her and you knew she wasn't going to come back. You had been driving around with her body in your truck for the last hour.

You're the first monster I've ever talked to.

#IAM911

Imagine Listening

Six months after the birth of the #IAM911 movement, I had an idea. I wanted to do something where I could give 9-1-1 dispatchers a chance to share their stories in a room full of their peers. It would be an hour-long session where in the first 30 minutes, they would have the opportunity to share out loud. Then, the second half of the session would allow them to share funny, light-hearted stories.

The session would be known as "Imagine Listening - Your worst day is our everyday..." I wanted to record the stories and share them on the podcast to shed even more light on what these heroes do and deal with. It was now 2017, six months later, and it was time to present this session at a public safety conference in Indiana. The room was packed, standing room only. A good friend of mine, Rob, assisted me, but I was nervous. I did not know what to expect as this was something that had never been done before. I completed my introduction and asked if anyone had a story to share. Not one person wanted to be the first.

I wasn't sure what to do. The success of this session depended on the participation of the attendees. I leaned forward and told the audience that if they wanted to write down their story and hand it up to my friend and I, we would read them out loud for them. Sheets of

paper were immediately ripped, passed, and attendees were writing. As they wrote, one person stood up, grabbed a microphone, and shared their story.

Tears streamed as the attendee spoke. After she finished, another person stood to speak. The session started out slow, but story after story was shared either out loud or written down. There was not a dry eye in the room. We were able to heal and find a form of closure through the power of storytelling. When it was time to share the funny stories, everyone was ready to laugh. This peer support session was a success.

Since that first session, Imagine Listening has been presented around the country at different public safety events. It is hard to explain to someone what it is like in a room where so much emotion is put into each story. I can only sum it up with one word. Powerful. The stories of those that make up the #IAM911 movement have been shared worldwide via the Within the Trenches podcast, and the impact has been great. I don't know that I will ever know the full impact of the movement and Imagine Listening, but I do have one story.

Years ago I received an anonymous message through social media. The author of the message said that they just wanted to thank the person who started this. Through our exchange, I found out that the person had been suicidal. They were scrolling through social media and stumbled upon the #IAM911 movement. This person read every single story in the photo album. After reading them, they no longer wanted to commit suicide. There were two reasons for this. First, the person didn't want their family to find them, and secondly, they didn't want to put the 9-1-1 dispatcher through that after reading how it sticks with them.

"I don't think you will ever know the impact of what you have created. Thank you."

This is how the conversation ended between myself and the anonymous writer. This interaction will always be with me and is proof of how important these stories are. It is true that one voice can make a difference, but in this case, the stories of the 9-1-1 professionals from all over the world are at the forefront of a new era, the era of the headset.

The #IAM911 movement continues...

Epilogue

Ricardo Martinez II founded the #IAM911 movement in 2016. However, the curtain to the world of 9-1-1 dispatch was opened in 2010 with "Behind the Mic - Stories from the Trenches." This was a college project where a story needed to be told as part of digital storytelling through music, narration, and still photos. Ricardo had struggled with 9-1-1 calls that he had buried but found it therapeutic to write about them. Because people had asked over and over what his craziest call was, he decided to educate the public by sharing his stories. For this project, however, he enlisted two co-workers to share the basics, how they got into dispatching, what was their worst and best call, and why they do what they do. A heartfelt shoutout goes to Whitney for her early contributions to the show, but especially to Trista and Alexis, who bravely shared their stories in 2010. It is the first version of what has become the Within the Trenches podcast, the #IAM911 movement, and Imagine Listening.

To find out more or share your #IAM911 story, visit **www.withinthetrenches.net**